the mirror trade

for Alan

the mirror trade
zoë skoulding

seren

Seren is the book imprint of
Poetry Wales Press Ltd
Nolton Street, Bridgend, Wales
www.seren-books.com

ISBN 1-85411-366-6

A CIP record for this title is available from the British Library.

The publisher acknowledges the financial assistance
of the Welsh Books Council.

Printed in Palatino by Gwasg Dinefwr, Llandybie.

Cover photograph: Angelika Röder.

Contents

In Certain Cities

There were days when cold
was so intense that words would freeze
in solid particles mid-air,
trajectories of shouts paralysed,
whispers textured in breeze,
murmurs left as moulded pebbles
suspended after the faces
had gone. Brushing ice in the quiet
we'd hear faint clicks
of syllables against shop windows,
a sudden clatter on a glass pavement.
We could only raise our arms
and shrug, deep in our furs,
baring our mouths to smile,
teeth icicled, lips blue,
or we'd just keep talking,
wondering what each phrase
would look like frozen –
till one by one they'd drop.

In spring you'd hear the shrieks
and chatter start to thaw
as vowels rose from meltpools
adrift from who or what or where,
and no-one answering.

Words Like Crystalline

They pass the planets seven, and pass the fixed,
And that crystalline sphere whose balance weighs
The trepidation talked, and that first moved.

Milton, *Paradise Lost*

Out here in the ninth sphere there's a serious wobble;
water's trembling to crash down in cataracts,
send the planets into swerves.
All this time its frozen quartz was ticking;

now I oscillate between the inside and the out,
these crystal lines like strands of glass,
a net for catching spooks, a body, generally solid.

And only words like *crystalline* will do for this,
the sense of being caught and held in ice
at the edge of everything you are or know.

*

When you look at me I'm all transduced,
planes of skin singing atoms at you, blood
swirled like wine. Cut glass. Drink me
only with your eyes.

And suddenly we're miles apart
across a table, lifting knives, weighing
their cold. *You don't know me.*
You think you do. You don't.

*

The crystalline lens lies behind the iris.
It lies. Light passes through it,

simple and exact, only to be
skewed, refracted, the bottom of the pool
not at all where you thought it was:
just go on, jump in, drown
in grey-green weeds converging
on a deep black well.

Ribbons of blood uncurl across the sclera;
the whole globe, held by tiny threads,
rolls in its orbit, meeting its double
only in mirrors, in glass, in water.

*

On Tuesday night the planets are aligned
but we won't see them through the cloud.
The spheres, though, they do make music
and it's full of crazy silences

or barely there as wineglass ring, a finger
balance on the outer rim. I'm walking
the perimeter of fields without a word when
wheels loop through the air, distant,

closer, their revolutions burning criss-
crossed trails. Then looking straight ahead you
slam out of the corner of one eye, too fast,
and I can't hold you there.

*

Your living daylights scare the darkness
down the underside to hide there. All this
is crystal and you're reading me in black and white.

Gas-permeable discs, flipped on with a fingertip
to cling like atmospheres, make everything so clear – as if
you could see right through me.

*

Now you're at the limit so keep running
on your optic nerve into jewels, ambiguities,
into the melted centre of the globe
where light is rivery – there is music
and you mustn't look back, no,
never even glance – deeper into
saline glitter, forgetting
skin, bone, what keeps us apart
as visions slant the surface,
edges curved, distorted, flattened figures
miming all this happening unseen
in the very far distance.

The Mirror Trade

Air shines. We snare it in our glass
with furnaces and transubstantiations,
quicksilver and tin amalgams.
We steal water from fire

then craft pure depth to capture space, annex
the country of illusions which looks in on us,
envying our every move,
always identical and opposite.

It's death to leave the island with this knowledge.
As we load mirrors, ships
bleed pictures of more ships
which lap the warehouse steps; we send out
pieces of ourselves which bear no trace of us.

Binocular

i.m. Peter Skoulding

As landscapes juddered, heavy on my nose,
catching glimpses of blurred bracken, rocks,

trees where I least expected them, I scanned
layers of blue, looking for you. Space

reeled in and out of focus; sky wobbled
uncertainly, or it might have been water.

I steadied my hands, inhaling stale leather,
the scuffed strap round my neck in case

I dropped them. Your military binoculars,
made to arrow to the point of threat

or target distant silhouettes, left me
giddy on the beach. Then all at once

there you are, sailing far out at sea,
so close that I can see the gleam of mackerel

in your hands. I move and the sea is empty.

The Naming of Binocular Bay

How he lost them on the beach I'll never know:
forties, Zeiss, a miracle of military optics
looted by his father in the aftermath

miles from this wind, this breath on my tongue,
seaspray hitting my skin like the spittle
of an old man trying to tell me –

He gave the bay their name, layered it
over the Ordnance Survey on his private map,
letters floating on a pale blue sea.

A cormorant dives headlong into glass,
its feathers spreading inkstains
as fish move invisibly, unidentified;

gulls dip and skim for nameless shadows
to be swallowed and forgotten
as I watch them through a Russian pair

with shaking tunnel vision, blinded by
smeared lenses, by what seems
to be in my grasp, two eyes fused
in a single open mouth.

Mostly Water

Coming down over Budapest
the plane's all eyes; dark spots
float up to stain the sky.

The wing dips over floods,
the tender land, as specks
of branches sweep downstream

and sun spills into crumpled
plastic on the breakfast trays.
Cold swells down my gullet

as I swallow bottled water,
as the Danube, flanked by crowds,
peristalsis of the city squeezing in,

rises to silence roads, stop doorways,
lifts itself from tints of grey
to turquoise, muscles up to blue.

Pupil

For Carol Skoulding

She would breathe in new print like anaesthetic
as words cut through to worlds she'd never known;

the library soothed playground wounds
with alphabetical order. Spines looked

down from shelves but each one blinked
its heart shut till she'd lift the cover,

tilting it towards the light. Now she watches
as a patient reads the letters on the wall:

W or Y - is that a T? Then M or X. She measures
for a lens to sharpen black on white. When the pupil

has turned milky she clips back an eyelid,
baring the cornea's edge for the glint of the knife.

Pause

My first language is silence and it edges
            into every sentence that I stutter, inserting clauses
of its own,   complicating
            what I tell you plainly. The air is full

            of voices, some of which
are mine. You can hear the press of them
            against your skull,   the clenching
of the brain against a mobile phone
            warm in your hand and pulsing
when you didn't   have anything to say
        anyway – I'm listening but all that's there is
            breath,   the hum of waves.

            The radio is tuning in
and out, each frequency a truth uncovered
        for a moment,   lost again. They're playing
your song in Siberia, one in the morning
        local time. The singer stops.   The song
runs on, arching into space until its radiating
        sighs and whispers   leave an empty circle
            for a voice to step into.

Birches

Out of the river's tape hiss,
the green drone of leaves, the wow
and flutter of wind

come trees like clean chimes
in echoed phrases falling
limb over limb,

cool fingers
rippling over skin
which peels away like paper,

sticking on words like
feeling and *silver*,
antique vowels

creaking into song
through gramophone crackle,
dust in the grooves.

Feet

Every footstep is a measurement,
the blind, iambic span of distances

that feet cannot escape. Percussive clicks
of heels across a polished floor become

a metronome to live by. Even when
they dance, not knowing themselves, or run

thumping to heartbeats, splay their toes in sand,
grip rock, hammer pavements, take great clawed

or cloven strides in dreams, the feet are counting
down. There's always one foot on the ground

or both. This is why angels fear to tread,
prefer to fly. And this is why, perhaps,

she's come to this last step: it's into air.

Airborne

It takes nerves of light,
        this suspension
in the invisible. To perform
        the Falling Leaf
the bi-plane flies straight up
        until it stalls, stops,
flutters twirling down,
        the engines restarting
at the last moment
        as she watches, upright
at ninety-six, a loop
        of pearls vapour-
trailed around her neck,
        silent in the roar
of planes shaking the glass,
        blood narrowed
to a blue throb
        and the sky still.

Feathers

No-one ever knew. A wreck, we thought,
a long way out at sea. We never found

another body, or any other trace;
the sea was a blank.

A foreigner, we were sure of it:
his mouth didn't look the right shape

to have spoken our language.
When we turned him over we found

scorch marks on his back as if
he had escaped a burning ship;

what clothes he wore were soaked in wax,
congealed about him,

cracked by waves. We guessed at candles –
frantic signalling at night,

emergency or lost direction. The feathers
we never understood, except

if we thought of a host of angels
abandoning the ship,

hot loops of their wings
beating towards the sun

or a cargo of geese set free
at the moment when hope was lost.

The Tailor of Ulm

Conversation was a low insect hum.
The mayor and guests arrived in a flutter of robes,
gleams of sunlight on silk. Expectation
floated on the currents of their breath;
the winged man flew, alone against the sky.

They'd seen his careful stitches,
the industrious construction of the frame
and wanted him to thread his way through blue,
rising till the Danube was a neat seam far below.
They saw him flying east forever,
almost heard the chimes of distant towers,
the babble of foreign tongues.

His plummet broke the spell.
The crowd unravelled,
disappointed at his tangles in the water,
remembering the last time the city
reached into the heavens:
that great cathedral spire
embroidered on the sky till gravity
tore gashes in it long ago
and ripped it down.

They took their tiny pathways home
as something between them rose
like the dreams of ants,
that dream of building it again.

Lobster

And here it is,
    after the circus trick of being sawn
        in two, grilled in mirrored halves
    cradled in shell.

All cusp,
    a creature wrapped in swaddling clothes
as if it could wriggle out –
    no, cut that and you're looking at
        insides, not interior,

the secret logic of the body
        gaping through cracks,
    eyes out on stalks.

Silence: an angel passes
        on twin wings:
    l'être-ange/l'étrange –
        ink-blue from another element.

The Shroud of Turin

Though carbon dating's blown the miracle,
that spring it haunted me. The explanation
was that the glow and scorch of resurrection
had made a holy photo possible,
a grainy cutting pasted in the Bible.
Over the smell of rot, grass shone.
Primroses turned their faces to the sun
along the path where gravestones grew as tall
as I was, their shadows longer. Birdsong bled
the certainties of winter. Curled up tight,
then wound in linen like a writhing bud,
I couldn't sleep, half-dreamed of monks all night
who'd marvel at the image I had seared
when fear had burned my arteries to light.

Transplants

Your kidney sings to mine
through skin and air. Our livers leap
like fish in wine-dark floods; four lungs
nestle together, folded wings rising
and falling to the same beat of blood.
A body becomes a home
before a country ever does.

*

Issei Sagawa – how she rolls
his name around her mouth,
celebrity cannibal-to-be
(after the gunshot and her silence).
Now he's getting right under her skin,
her body open, every juncture losing
meaning, tissue torn apart, fissures
in the flesh, this puzzling absence –
and all he wanted was
the light that came from her.

*

There's rain outside, a wind
that sends everybody mad.
Drenched in seconds, water
streaming down my neck,
I'm on the doorstep
fumbling with the key

while waves consume
the land which crumbles
at their touch; it was only sand
and now it's shifted into masses under sea.
Foreign matter sluices in, the alien
salts and fishscales, broken glass
which once held liquids we wouldn't
know the names of, intoxicating
tides which wash away
the sand, the soil, which lighten us.

By the Time He Gets to Nant y Benglog

By the time he gets to Nant y Benglog
I'll be shifting my head on the pillow,
feeling the weight of dreams unclog
as a stream of ants comes pouring through
the bleached rim of my left eye.

By the time he gets to Pentrefoelas
the blue light from the curtains will be
turning me green. As dawn uncoils
I'll look down from this body
sprawling here, soaring and steep.

By the time he gets to Cerrigydrudion
I'll sink further into sleep,
filling his empty space like a stone
dropped into water: soundless, deep,
leaving ring on ring on the surface.

By the time he gets to Froncysyllte
I'll be reaching the crossing place
as the spool of night begins to stutter
and snap. He'll feel the threads between us
stretch as thin as B roads on his map.

Britannia Bridge

Now you feel the edge of silence
as a surface tension, meniscus stretched

to breaking point. Traffic booms
overhead, its weight suspended;

power looped across the Straits by pylons –
fission, fire, wind and water – gathers

into high wires too slack to dance along,
lines heavy with too much meaning.

M1, M6, A55, A5, the fluid gesture
of the Intercities sweeping west

and east – it's the kind of touch
from which there's no retreat. Already

the Coppola remake runs and runs:
shore thick with greeny darkness,

heart throbbing for the helicopters,
Wagner over water, that apocalyptic flame.

The Aztecs of Cwm Llan

Light is obsidian knives, the sun in splinters
on a pyramid of slate; copper
stains the scree to sunset

from some forgotten
ripping out of hearts.

At the ruins of the temple of the cwm
Madoc's people chat
in fluent Nahuatl.

Gladstone dodders on the rock, bringing
tears to the eyes of quarrymen
while everybody sings

and goes on singing, mouths
full of earth.

Through Trees

circled by gull
shrieks slicks of
mud sucking at
feet banded sky
black trees this
shaking palm of
ruffled grey-blue
water jolts foot
steps closer you
have to go with
what's   coming
in a flutter of
oyster-catchers
over water and
blood flowering
under skin tuned
to concert pitch
then   wavering
slowly   off-key
in   frequencies
your ears will
never catch as
bones pile up
problems for the
future   muscles
waste chances &
fat builds up for
nothing but to
bulk this column
raised in honour
of human futility

trees print on skin
a   birch   kiss
burns shadow on
your   epidermis
flushed by wind
or sun peeling
slightly   scratch
off to reveal the
winning answers
all   correct   but
the prize out of
your grasp like
the whole ethical
trouble involved
in wearing some-
one   else's   face
rather than heart
a light wind rises
& a momentary
shiver raises new
knots   a   second
scars you change
scores a surface
wrinkle   trunks
lean into others
for   safety   in
likeness to build
a   paper   tower
everyone   must
agree quickly on
the best method

a sharp frost in
Pentraeth woods
each leaf edged in
white in your
memory of 1992
Duisburg in the
snow you set out
without knowing
how far from one
lost street to
another through
such trees how
far from there to
here & now you
are a pillar of
salt your slow
erosion in rain a
bitter crumbling
of your bones a
series of wooden
poses held in
wired anatomies
the head tilted to
look back frozen
to a pose dried
out in deserts
parched seabeds
snow that never
comes any more
the trees' harsh
angles falter fall

each breath sifts
air for salt soft
rot to heave a
blush of oxygen
into its hollows
on Llanddwyn
beach a red
balloon is rooted
in dune grasses
its taut string
pulls air tight
against air you
gulp at the sky
vaulted vapour in
this movement
perpetual over
the globe fiery
mobile & lucid
it haunts you at
the core a deep
gap shot through
with fizz white
foam seethes at
the waves' edge
breath traverses
you as if words
come puffed out
forced panting
from these gapes
in the self & its
very own stink

you're all water
through larches
the steep path
rises past fallen
trees uprooted
limbs sunk in
mud roots torn a
gaping mouth of
underworld you
listen across the
river to all that
you've forgotten
high fierce voice
the gesture of a
hand this stream
of ice shivers a
stalactite forms
his single look
forbidden what
you were hangs
in a slant of rain
your eye glint
varnished to an
ooze of Prussian
blue you curl the
tube of paint
pressed to its
crimped edge
that voice it
turned you to
liquid every time

bracelet of bright
about bone yours
or mine these
pointless protein
traces you were
what you ate &
high in the holly
the birds made
their nests gold
with clipped hair
fallen in the
spring garden a
covering like
water falling in
whose eyes as
one rises above
the other in a
tangle of DNA
this is all that's left
of you now
a bottled high
gloss shimmer
reconstructing a
well-conditioned
human being just
wash in & leave
for two minutes
wash out rain
pelts grey sheen
over long grass
bleached white

Undergrowth

'Stop!' says the forest the wolf comes out of
roots bruised by footsteps, crushed under wheels;

a blurred pelt slips from the edge of eyes
and leaves us in a fug of berries, mulch.

So what if I won't let you in on my private thoughts
when paths multiply a forest's disregard for boundaries –

lightning-fractured bark comes away in your hand
revealing beetle journeys, hunger, wandering script –

I crossed left, right, curved back on myself
perhaps a dozen times, maybe more,

pen over page a broken trail of ink, or every key
another step towards the bottom right-hand corner.

From here it's a matter of tracking with night goggles
as insects drive you back, each pinpoint stab

a red blotch of incursion or means of getting by
like alder saplings pushing out of fallen spruce

or lichen graffiti in the broadleaf zone.
Electronic sensors blink at the edge of a continent

where lime and hornbeam flash citrus to green amber,
lining a species corridor for boar calling boar, elk

dreaming of elk across the border, the barrier
across the road just a stop on the way through.

City in the Intermediate Realm

Poem from a title by Paul Klee

Between ground and sky
its streets unfold a crumpled
plan of another city,
one you haven't been to

where cafés fade in smoke
behind peeling plaster
with bullet holes suspended
in fractions of a second

which will not pass.
The eyes of strangers
swerve out into traffic but
their scent swoops close,

vanishes in the river's
damp stench. You cross
the bridge which trembles
slightly when your feet

fall into a rhythm of patches:
ochre, dove, sepia, steel,
changing like snatches overheard
of languages you instantly forget.

Chartres

The guard announced: *L'univers a changé.*
The train slowed into Versailles-Chantiers,
weather shifting as we rumbled into cloud

and out again and on through miracles
you couldn't see for green. It's so easy
to lose exact meanings in transition.

A labyrinth snaked the floor of the cathedral,
false paths as polished as true:
a thousand footsteps in the wrong direction.

The only way was up, a spiral into
tangled masonry so high you'd swear
it moved in wind; gargoyles spat rain

and headless dogs chased saints. Everywhere
the buttresses perfected their translations
of the whole weight of the stone and flew.

Sous les Pavés, La Plage

A voice sings: *Ne pleure pas Marilou*
deep in the Metro's black throat,
rises through the grind of trains,

wells up and bursts through cobbled streets.
Thin trees in rain are shaken
to the sap. Houses shiver

as the voice floods attic rooms,
inundations breaking into waves, surfacing
above the rooftops where the chimneys float,

the Sacré Coeur a beached white whale
under a paved sky.

Paris: Ghosts at No. 9

it's an empty street it's
full of figures moving
while the dream machine
ripples strips of dark
interfering with his alpha
waves the ghosts of number nine
are restless *sous les pavés*

the beach at Tangier is a turning page
windswept over-exposed the colours
bleached the chief effects
of a dirty bomb are fear and panic
increased incidence of cancer

interposition of curves the ghosts
are interfering with each other
salts feared and panic greater
below the agitated stones the phantoms
of the new mingle with us shaken

underneath the streets' whitened
vacuum a bleached beach the feared
is cupping glasses the grass of panic in
windy curves his name again empty
rotation movable bodies incidental cancer

the street empties
agitation mingles with the dirt
fear shaken in a glassy wind the steady
flick of light and dark disrupting
the stones Tangier is underneath
bodies incidental on the beach

The Bridge

Berlin, 2000

It's not so much what's there as what isn't:
the strip of forest where the trees have not yet grown,
the concrete bridge connecting roads which have
vanished under leaves.

The absence runs on, stopping at nothing,
cutting through roads and rivers, pavements and houses,
sometimes visible as a cobbled suture,
a seam between the world as it was
and the city as it is;

it's a faultline through Potsdamer Platz
where the buildings have pushed down roots
faster than trees, binding old rifts with
steel threads and sky-high glass.

At dusk, the bridge is an apparition in the woods.
A sound like the skitting of dry leaves becomes
a shaken spray can. The bridge
is the only thing that's left to paint,
but the lone boy has no slogans, nothing more to say,
except to make his sign for himself
over and over again.

Journey on Good Friday

This train, rattling down split
zygotes, lines veering into the edges

of palms held up to catch the
blossom which clouds the stark

connections of the branches
above the pond where tadpoles

houdini out of jelly into murk
the colour of these windows

open for extra ventilation
as the chain of lights curves through

all the carriages like mirrors
reflecting to infinity,

it is going one way only, west.

Westminster

And the hapless Soldier's sigh
Runs in blood down Palace walls
William Blake

When they turned
the soldiers into stone
and scrubbed the buildings
clean, they left guns
pointing at all angles, frozen

crossfire turning savagely
trimmed grass into a void
where enemies make
and remake themselves,
all bright and glittering.

Uruk

He could make men laugh or cry
by pronouncing the word
Mesopotamia

printed on a flyleaf map
    pressed down on a civilisation
    of onion skin,
    hand on maroon calf –
        the whole truth and nothing but.

Our horrible blue eyes:
sky shining through the sockets
    of an empty skull.

To deconflict an airspace
you have to think in four dimensions,
        three you know
then all the possible trajectories.

Scored lines in clay converge
        in twenty-four hour satellite
pictographs to tally sacks of corn
while Uruk crumbles;
a pattern of raised surfaces
        rewrites itself in dust.

Klimt's Buchenwald

Beech Forest was an innocent name
when he chose it, as light as slender trees
spattered with gold, patterning a clear horizon.

Loading his brush with crimson
to fleck dead leaves into the ground,
he didn't have to see that colour
seeping into earth.

Painting pale verticals
he couldn't have been thinking
of fifty-six thousand ghosts
or the roots of the trees and how they might
probe and shatter concrete chambers,
tangle with hidden bones;

the rhythm of lines is the sound of a waltz,
not the slow chug of trains to their termination.

This is an entirely different forest, where the beeches
dance blindly to the sun and only one dark trunk
leans forward, a stained word.

Eclipse

The boxes in the cafe show it all in original 3D.
You fit your eyes to two round lenses in the wood,
focus, and the past sharpens. You could almost
limp into the trench with the men who carry
that shrouded body. After a moment you see
how it's missing from the chest up.

You can drive for miles through fields which still
explode each time they're ploughed, the earth
still white and heavy, clinging to your feet in lumps.

Keep watching the skies for signs and portents:
everyone knows where the future's coming from.
Families with welding shields and matching mirror specs
gaze up in one direction, B-movie extras in a scene
where everybody's awestruck in the mud while the sun
hauls itself along with its jaw shot away.

Suddenly it all slides into perspective
as you see how far away the sun is, how black,
how next time you will be absent.

November 5 p.m.

On the moon you'd pass
from brightness into black

with nothing spilled or blurred.
Wrapped in vapour, lensed

like a lost eye, these hemispheres
are ringed with dusk,

its slow tide of reversals
bringing absences

of mice skitting in a dark kitchen,
the visitors you semi-glimpse

through strands of hair
you brush aside, forgetting

half the world's invisible.
At this rim the gleam is doubled,

split, a mirror you could
plunge your hands through,

watching bracelets of glass
circle your wrists

until a switch in time flicks on
the glare of screens.

Optimistic Poem

We've been divided since the world began:
we hope or dread. All of us blindly stumble.
Things can't get any worse. Oh yes they can.

The skies explode; the broadcaster is deadpan
as we watch disaster strike, the mighty humbled.
We've seen it coming since the world began,

we pessimists, our heads out of the sand
so irony can't touch us. By all means grumble
as things can't get any worse. Oh yes, they can

appear to but imagination spans
the worst before the real does more than rumble.
We've felt no different since the world began:

it's cancer or it's anthrax, famine, gunman,
fire or fall-out. We've seen the future crumble.
Not knowing would be worse, oh yes. You can

tell us nothing for which we haven't planned;
we have no hopes, which means they can't be tumbled.
We've been waiting since the world began
to see if things could be worse, and now they can.

Trappist Brewers

They smile and glide as if time means nothing,
as if there are no billboards outside the sleepy town
showing how Chimay is drunk in Tokyo.

From their glassed-in cloisters they remember
how power, prayer and alcohol flooded the veins
of the oldest maps. The road from the abbey leads

to the town square, where bells ring out of tune,
tinny and distinct, marking out
each quarter hour while nothing changes.

Wild rabbit from the fields below melts
into plums and onions; the cheese is creamy,
dipped in salt. Remembering that rich, slow drunkenness

back home, I'll buy the same beer under
bland fluorescent light
and drink it from the wrong glass,

searching its bitter velvet for a footstep on stone,
an off-key chime or a white scut
disappearing into the woods.

Voda

Medzilaborce, Slovakia

Turn on the tap and *voda* splutters
brownish consonants. Slipping

from the banks of sleep to vodka
singing at three in the morning,

the same phrase repeated
down by the river, I can believe

in speech gritted by earth,
flecked with belonging

to a place that everybody leaves.
The bright hotel which teeters

by the bridge, painfully new –
its corridors whisper

International, all alone
in this town, where *voda* is *voda*

and couldn't be anything else,
could it? But they're still singing

that one line over and over
as if the rest of it escapes them, as if

they just can't reach that spring from which
the muddy floods of song might burst.

Old Money

That party trick, neat origami folds
to turn the Queen and Dickens into McEnroe

won't work on new tenners. Darwin is
immutable, his eyes turned from the Beagle

distant on the smooth horizon.
He's bearded, full of gravitas, like a cousin

of Pedro Alvereo Cabral, who sailed
each thousand escudos to a pale Brazil

of geometric jungles, startled parrots
and monkeys mad with fright. *Banco de Portugal*:

the ship arrived with rays of flame behind it
fanned out like a wad of crumpled promises

filthy with sweat and traces of cocaine,
each one two-faced and greedy as a gene.

Gibraltar

The little neck of sea is difficult
for submarines to slide through undetected;
all night you dream of the drip
drip on metal, the immense pressure of water
and the eyes of the enemy.

Two continents stretch out their fingertips
but don't quite touch. We can see Africa,
we can see it clearly.

In a small room in a narrow lane
you steer my finger through the ring,
then we escape, blinking into sunlight.

On the empty runway we pose together
while a stranger takes a photo
and my white dress is a sail
lifted by the wind.

Taxi Driver, Delhi

He does not drive, but swerves,
    every movement an avoidance
        of truck, cow, Mercedes, beggar.

He has learnt how to breathe
    in this substance which is not air
        but something grey and choking

laced with diesel, jasmine, sewage, incense;
    how, when the owner of a towering four-by-four
        shakes his fist and shouts

through the open window,
    to raise one hand in blessing, mutter:
        Shantih, shantih, shantih.

Sleeping Inside

Letter to my Grandfather

Wiping jam from your fingers, you scan the copperplate,
the stamp of King George over Rameswaran Temple.
You rip it open with your silver blade.

I beg to inform about your mess Abdul and Lt Green's Bearer
both men spoil the name of all the officers

You sip your tea. Perhaps you take another piece of toast
and cut it carefully in two, then polish clean your knife
by slicing it inside the bread.

they are quarrelling one day and abusing using very bad word
which I cannot repeat in your respect.

I can almost see your slightly crooked smile – the one
I have inherited – at this broken version of your tongue.
You laugh and read it to your wife:

Both men are very proud they are also fighting in civil court
which your honour well know. These men are not suitable in
your mess

You gaze out vaguely at the lawn, the hired shrubs.
It's far too hot out there already. You remember
that it's almost time to book your passage home.

you are great judges and you can judgement yourself.
I beg to remain, sir, your most obedient...

What would the wise king do?
Cut the baby in half. Divide. Rule. You adjust
your spectacles and feel like Solomon himself.

Sleeping Inside

This is the silly season. There are dust storms
and no sign yet of rain. I'm not sleeping
outside on the lawn, despite the heat.
Safer inside, what with all the trouble.
They all come down our road. Down from Amritsar
with their daggers. In the mess last night
while we were playing slosh we heard some shouting.
Moslems and Sikhs. Several dead. Lahore
was like Manhattan in that film *King Kong*,
so Wardle says. Crowds screamed and ran.
Good job the wife's still in the hills. Tonight
everything is quiet; I still can't sleep.
Too hot. The room is shadows on a screen;
black flickers across my eyelids. Something
dark and massive grips me and I'm swept
up to terrifying heights, blanched
and helpless, clenched in this enormous fist.

Tombs

We rode in a tonga to the tombs
through a blaze of mustard
past ruins crumbling into dust

which settled everywhere unbidden.
Beneath it, Thelma's skin
was flaking off in patches

to reveal a raw, bright red.
Her parasol was indispensable.
We stood on balconies

shaded by broken traceries of stone,
framed views through ogee windows.
Who'd think that empires when they're dead

can leave detritus such as this?
At sunset Thelma said we should go back,
her arms a spreading rash, a blotched pink map.

North West

There were rumours of bears
in the valley: paw prints, blood marks,
blurs between boulders.

Sand devils blow the hangars
down again. Musa Khan's incursions
keep us on our toes.

We took a nullah each,
scrambling over loose wood,
cracking branches. This was
bear country, without a doubt.

I break my glasses playing tennis.
Almighty nuisance. One lens smashed
and the distance is a haze.

I fired one shot. It must have been
a shadow, not a bear.

Bombing gets off to a roaring start
with fifty hits.

I was beginning to believe
that there were no bears in Kashmir.

On the aerodrome
two aeroplanes collide,
blinded by a cloud of dust.
A nice mess. Two write-offs
but no-one hurt.

At last. I saw them for a moment:
a female and two cubs, close enough
to hear them shuffle through the leaves,
but still no luck.

Machine gun raids all day. Just
swoop low and fire. We know
exactly where they are.

All night in our tents
the air was still. We listened
for the bears, the skies
shot through with bullet holes of light.

Arak in Mesopot

You have to be careful with arak,
its delayed action, its effect
of delaying action.

Poor Selby – went completely native,
certainly bats. The mail had just come in –
bad news? Who knows. Living here's enough.

Listen to the wind in the eucalyptus trees –
that antiseptic scent.
Fresh air is the thing, if you can get it.

The day we flew out to the desert,
the arch of Ctesiphon,
I was in control, swooping down
over the lone and level sands;

Selby, ready with his camera, aiming,
firing at a haze. The heat.
The great vault from that height
like a shattered skull –

however, the poor chap's dead
and there's a mess to be cleared up.

Bazaar

In the broken buildings
monkeys swing like cats.
I haggle over carpets,
buy a dagger and some bangles,
but I'm well and truly
puggled by the heat.

Come, sit. The fortune teller
has me in his palm. I listen.
My collar itches.
He's gabbling about birds:
egrets, peacocks, parrots, crows.
Vultures, he says, and his eyes
cloud over. In them I can see
flocks of birds making
shadows on the land,
their feathers falling –

and then I see I'm
one of them. I tilt my wings,
look down on the city's
heaps of rubble, ant hills,
miniature minarets.
Babus clutch umbrellas,
thinking of thunder
and underneath me rugs of woven silk
unroll in endless patterns.

Trans-Siberian, 1927

His letter from Shanghai, his seventh, reaches
Tientsin at dawn. *Dearest Madge...*
Already he's forgotten what he's written.
He polishes his shoes until he sees his face in them.

No coin here is genuine unless it's stamped.
There are three kinds of dollar which are often
counterfeit. Real Chinese money is the tael,
a silver, boat-shaped coin one never sees.

From Ulan-Ude to Irkutsk, the train
circles Baikal. Fishing trawlers plumb
transparency, cut through clouds which swim
the surface. The letter's curling in its sack.

There are chits for almost everything,
even laid out in the pews at church –
you fill in what you want to give –
end of the month they all come home to roost.

From Novosibirsk, empty trees
give way to empty trees. Her letter
(if only you could see the roses now)
number five, crosses his at Omsk.

Last night we went out to the Carlton. You buy
a book of tickets, give one for each dance
to the hostesses, mostly Russian girls.
I danced with one who wore her hair like yours.

A guard leafs through *Pravda*. The train pulls
slowly out of Moscow, on to Paris.
Young soldiers watch themselves dissolve
through glass into cyrillic blurs.

At the Dressing Table

you learn command, rehearsing rage
chilled to a silver calm, caught
on my surface, this dead river,
the one which keeps you from home,
the one which keeps you from them,
the one you'll sail across
with annas on your eyes.

Sacking the servants (ayah,
bearer, cook) took all the skill
you've learned from me,
the only one you trust.
How could I deceive you?
If I tell you right is left,
and left is right, it is because here,
they are. Lift me at arm's length
to face my double and I can show you
how you look when your back's
turned, when they whisper.

Let me surprise you with a face
you hardly recognise, a form
in duplicate, a chit, the currency
of paper skin: it's all you own.

Behind you, through the window
in the corner of an eye you catch
the bowed shapes of those who leave you,
their anger lowered against the sun,
taking slow steps out of your sight.

A History of the Andaman Islands

You are Marco Polo.
The island is arrows and eyes,
tongues of creeper licking
round the trees. You see
a most brutal and savage race,
having heads resembling those
of the canine species.
Every person, not being of their own nation,
whom they can lay their hand upon,
they kill and eat.

You are a doctor. You are
thinking of Lucknow, Lahore, Calcutta,
reading Marco Polo to the convicts
while sea washes over coral
and infinite white sand. Freedom
is a sickness you can cure:
you feed them medicine, grain by grain
until they sicken. You find judicious use
of flogging beneficial.

You are Prisoner 68.
The ocean which surrounds you
is *kalapani*, your black water,
across which there is no return.
Eternity is cellular. Shadows glance
through corridors, shafts of sunlight
through grilles. You swim the dark,
weightless against the rubber tube –
It's for your own good –
until they drown you in milk.

You are English, a doctor's wife.
Your mother thought you mad
to come here but you eat iced prawns
and dance under salmon-pink bougainvillaea,
coral beads against your small white neck.
The mountain is called Harriet. You love
to watch the sunset from her summit
as the world turns rosy.

Adela's Elephant

Here comes that elephant again, swaying
across the lawn as if she owned the place.
Grasmere has never seen the like!

Her flank's a wall of stone which blocks the view
I used to love. I can't get far enough
away to focus. The doctor's hands are kind;

they made me think of yours, of skin on skin
dissolving everything. He soothes
the elephant. Don't ask me how she got here:

too vast, too painted, she looks in on me
as if I'm hollow tracery, a figure
on a frieze, as if she's trying to see

the real me, who's hidden in a cave,
who has become a cave, where echo on echo's
calling someone else's name.

Mussoorie Walk

When I walk along that path
(in mist, the outlines of trees
twisted in incomprehensible script)

dudhwallahs pass like ghosts
which I can hardly see,
blinded by this whiteness

as I slip, grasping, at nothing,
jolt down the *kudh*, snagging
on roots and branches, to wake –

the words I want are
white spaces eating through
continents of language,
undiscovering them.

Notes

The Mirror Trade
The secrets of the Venetian mirror industry, of which Sabine Melchior-Bonnet's *The Mirror: A History* gives an account, were once closely guarded on the island of Murano.

Lobster
The angelic/uncanny pun is Jacques Lacan's.

Transplants
Issei Sagawa has been the subject of several TV documentaries; the italicised line in the second stanza is direct quotation of Sagawa explaining his motives.

Undergrowth
The first line is from Michel de Certeau.

Sous Les Pavés, La Plage
The title is taken from situationist graffiti which was revived in Paris in May, 1968. The song in the first line is by Serge Gainsbourg.

Paris Ghosts at No. 9
The title is from a film by Anthony Balch in collaboration with William Burroughs, Brion Gysin and Ian Somerville. The poem was developed by putting sections of the text through French and Spanish translation software and back into English.

Uruk
Uruk, now in Iraq, is thought to have been the first city and the place where writing was invented. The third stanza is adapted from T. E. Lawrence's *Seven Pillars of Wisdom*.

Sleeping Inside
The first seven of these poems make extensive use of letters and diaries of Frank Skoulding, my grandfather, from his time in the R.A.F. in India, Iraq and China in the twenties and thirties.

A History of the Andaman Islands
From 1858 to 1939 The British Raj sent Indian dissidents and muti-
neers to an island penal colony where torture, forced labour and
medical experimentation were routine. I have drawn on research
and interviews with survivors published in an article by Cathy
Scott-Clark and Adrian Levy in *The Guardian*, June 2001.

Westminster
The last line is from Wordsworth's 'Composed Upon Westminster
Bridge'.

Adela's Elephant
This draws on E.M. Forster's *A Passage to India*.

Mussoorie Walk
Dudhwallahs: milkmen
Kudh: hillside

Acknowledgements

Some of the poems, or earlier versions of them, have appeared in the following publications: *Magma, Oxygen* (seren, 2000), *The Pterodactyl's Wing* (Parthian 2003), *Poetry London, Planet, Poetry Wales, Rattapallax, The Rialto, Shearsman.*